JBIOG
Caesa 04-4-07
Reid, Struan

Julius Caesar

Historical Biographies

JULIUS CAESAR

Struan Reid

Heinemann Library
Chicago, Illinois

© 2002 Reed Educational & Professional Publishing
Published by Heinemann Library,
an imprint of Reed Educational & Professional Publishing,
Chicago, Illinois

Customer Service 888-454-2279

Visit our website at www.heinemannlibrary.com

Designed by Celia Floyd
Illustrated by Jeff Edwards and Joanna Brooker
Originated by Ambassador Litho Ltd
Printed by Wing King Tong in Hong Kong

06 05 04 03 02
10 9 8 7 6 5 4 3 2 1

Library of Congress Cataloging-in-Publication Data
Reid, Struan.
  Julius Caesar / Struan Reid.
     p. cm. -- (Historical biographies)
Includes bibliographical references and index.
Summary: Presents an account of Julius Caesar's life, from birth to
death, and explores his impact on history and the world.
  ISBN 1-58810-564-4 (HC), 1-58810-999-2 (Pbk.)
  1. Caesar, Julius--Juvenile literature. 2. Heads of
state--Rome--Biography--Juvenile literature. 3.
Generals--Rome--Biography--Juvenile literature. 4.
Rome--History--Republic, 265-30 B.C.--Juvenile literature. [1. Caesar,
Julius. 2. Heads of state. 3. Generals. 4. Rome--History--Republic,
265-30 B.C.] I. Title. II. Series.
  DG261 .R45 2002
  937'.05'092--dc21

                                  2001003659

Acknowledgments
The author and publishers are grateful to the following for permission to reproduce copyright material:
Cover photograph: Scala
pp. 4, 7, 12, 24, 28 Scala; pp. 6, 14, 18, 19, 22, 23 Ancient Art and Architecture; p. 8 Trevor Clifford;
pp. 9, 26, 29 AKG; pp. 10, 15 British Museum; p. 11 Corbis; pp. 13, 16, 17, 20, 25, 27 The Art Archive;
p. 21 Montreal Museum of Fine Arts.

Special thanks to Rebecca Vickers for her comments in the preparation of this book.

Every effort has been made to contact copyright holders of any material reproduced in this book.
Any omissions will be rectified in subsequent printings if notice is given to the publisher.

Some words are shown in bold, **like this.** You can find out what they mean by looking in the glossary.

Many Roman names and terms may be found in the pronunciation guide.

Contents

Who Was Julius Caesar?

Julius Caesar was a Roman **politician** and general who lived more than 2,000 years ago. He was perhaps one of the most **ambitious** men who has ever lived. He would let nothing get in the way of his climb to power.

Rome in Caesar's time

In the time of Julius Caesar, Rome was one of the most powerful states in the Western world. It had been governed as a **republic** for 400 years. By the time of his death, he held the most powerful position that the Roman Republic had ever seen. He introduced many changes to the way Rome and its **empire** were ruled, many of which remained in place for the next 500 years.

Stabbed to death

Caesar's ambitions eventually became too much for the other political families of Rome, and he was stabbed to death by a group of politicians. By then, the days of the Roman Republic were already numbered. Julius Caesar had made so many changes to the government that it could never return to the way it had been run. His work was continued by his adopted son, Octavian, who eventually became the first Roman **emperor**.

▼ Julius Caesar rose to become the most powerful man in Rome and changed the course of world history forever.

How do we know?

We know about Julius Caesar and about ancient Roman **civilization** from the writings and records the Romans kept. Very few original Roman books and papers have survived, but we do have later copies made by **monks** and **scholars.** These include works of history, **politics,** and **philosophy,** as well as plays, poems, and letters. Other information comes from stone **inscriptions** and Roman coins.

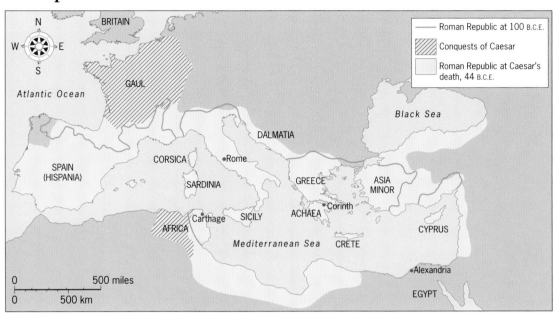

▲ This map shows the extent of the Roman Republic at the time of Julius Caesar's birth in about 100 B.C.E., and at his death in 44 B.C.E. During that time, the empire expanded far beyond the shores of the Mediterranean Sea.

Key dates

About 100 B.C.E.	Birth of Julius Caesar
63 B.C.E.	Caesar is made chief priest of Rome
58–50 B.C.E.	Caesar's **campaigns** in Gaul
45 B.C.E.	Caesar becomes **dictator** for life, and ruler of the Roman world
44 B.C.E.	Death of Julius Caesar

Watch the dates

"B.C.E." after a year date means before the common era. This is used instead of the older abbreviation "B.C." The years are counted backwards toward zero.

Caesar's Early Life

Gaius Julius Caesar was born around the twelfth day of Quinctilis (later renamed July, after him) in about 100 B.C.E. His father, also named Gaius Julius Caesar, was a government official called a **praetor**. His mother, Aurelia, came from an old and powerful noble family. His father's family, known as the Julii, was also very ancient and claimed to be descended from the goddess Venus.

Caesar's parents were not very rich, and he grew up with a strict, plain family life. They lived in Rome. There were some household servants, such as maids, cooks, and **slaves.** Aurelia had a nursemaid to help her raise her son and his two younger sisters.

▲ This wall painting from a house in the town of Pompeii shows what the inside of a Roman house would have looked like.

School days

Like the sons of most noble families, Caesar was educated by a private **tutor** from a young age. When he was about eleven years old, he was probably sent to a secondary school, called a *grammaticus,* where he studied subjects such as history, **philosophy**, geography, mathematics, **astronomy**, and music. He was also taught the Greek language by a man named Antonius Gnipho.

Greek was one of the most important subjects at school. Greek **culture** had a very strong influence on the Romans, since they had inherited their religion and much of their way of life from the Greeks. Greek and Roman literature was studied in great detail, and students were expected to learn whole passages by heart.

▶ Young men who wanted to become **politicians** needed to master the art of **oratory,** or public speaking. They were taught how to write speeches properly and how to present them well.

Preparing for public service

Because Julius Caesar was born into a **patrician** family, he was expected to have a career in **politics** or in the army. To do this, he had to learn to speak in public. From the age of about thirteen, he was sent to a teacher of public speaking, called a *rhetor.*

Growing Up in Rome

In 85 B.C.E., when Caesar was about sixteen years old, his father died. As the new head of the family, he was left to look after his mother and two younger sisters.

The following year, Caesar officially became an adult at a ceremony attended by many other young men from noble families.

A useful marriage

It was normal for Roman parents to choose husbands and wives for their children. While he was still a boy, Caesar's father had chosen a future bride for him, named Cossutia. When his father died, Caesar broke off the engagement. Instead, he married a woman named Cornelia. She was the daughter of Cinna—one of the most powerful men in Rome. Their wedding was in about 84 B.C.E., and their daughter, Julia, was born about a year later.

▲ The Forum was a large square in the center of Rome. It contained many of the city's most important buildings. It was there that Caesar officially became an adult. These ruins are all that is left today.

Forced into hiding

With his powerful new family connections, Caesar began to climb up the ladder to power. He became an officer in the army and also held a junior position in the government. But in 82 B.C.E., when he was about eighteen, Caesar's world was shattered.

In that year, a **politician** named Sulla came to power. Sulla viewed Caesar as a threat to his authority and tried to have the young man murdered. Caesar was forced to go into hiding in the hills outside Rome.

▶ Lucius Cornelius Sulla was the leader of one of the Roman political parties. His ideas were opposed to those that Caesar's family supported.

The Roman Republic

Rome was a **republic**, meaning that its rulers were elected by the **citizens**. The most important citizens, called **patricians**, belonged to the old noble families. Only patricians were allowed to become members of the **Senate**, the group of people who decided how Rome was governed.

A Greek Adventure

After several months in hiding, Caesar was pardoned by Sulla and allowed to return to Rome. Even so, he decided that it would be wise to stay away. In 80 B.C.E., he served as a soldier in Greece under the command of a general named Minucius Thermus. Caesar was awarded an important military decoration, called the *corona civica*, for his part in the capture of the city of Mitylene on the island of Lesbos.

A skillful speaker

In 78 B.C.E., Sulla died, and it was safe for Caesar to return to Rome. He earned a reputation as a skilled **orator** when he acted as a lawyer at the trial of an old friend of Sulla's. Although Caesar did not win the case, his performance made him famous.

Captured by pirates

In 76 B.C.E., when he was about 24, Caesar decided to travel to the Greek island of Rhodes to study under a famous **philosopher**, Apollonius Molon. On the way, his ship was captured by **pirates**, and Caesar was taken to the island of Pharmacusa (modern Farmakonisi).

▶ A Roman soldier wore a metal helmet and an armored tunic and leg guards, and carried a shield. He fought with a spear, sword, and dagger.

The pirates demanded a **ransom** of twenty gold **talents**—a huge sum of money. Caesar told them he was worth at least 50 talents! He also told them that as soon as he was released he would be back to kill them. After six weeks, the ransom was paid, and Caesar was set free. He immediately sailed back to Pharmacusa and had all the pirates executed.

▲ Caesar was traveling to the Greek island of Rhodes, just off the western coast of Turkey, when he was attacked by pirates.

Pirate attacks

Pirates were a constant danger to ships in the Mediterranean Sea. Although the Romans ruled many of the lands around the Mediterranean, they did not control the sea itself. Their ships were often attacked by pirates. The Romans were not able to put an end to piracy for many years.

Growing Power

The story of Caesar's capture by **pirates** ensured that his name now became even more famous back in Rome. The **citizens** of Rome were beginning to regard Caesar as a very strong leader.

The push for power

Caesar returned to Rome in 73 B.C.E., and now, at about age 27, he began his real push for power. He used his family connections to open as many doors as he could. For example, his appointed position as a priest of Jupiter allowed him to meet many important people. In 69 B.C.E., he was elected to the post of military **tribune**. Although this was not a very important job, it was a useful step up the ladder to power.

In 68 B.C.E., Caesar was elected to the junior post of *quaestor* for one year, and went to work in Spain. This was a very remote posting. Maybe some other **politicians** were growing alarmed at Caesar's lust for power and wanted to get him out of the way.

▶ As a priest of Jupiter, Caesar would have been expected to take part in ceremonies at a temple like this, the Temple of Fortuna Virilis in Rome.

A new wife

Before he left Rome for Spain, Caesar's wife, Cornelia, died from an illness. On his return the next year, he married again. His new wife, Pompeia, was the cousin of a famous general named Gnaeus Pompeius Magnus (usually known as Pompey), and the granddaughter of Caesar's old enemy, Sulla. She was also extremely rich—a quality that would be very useful in helping Caesar buy his way into power.

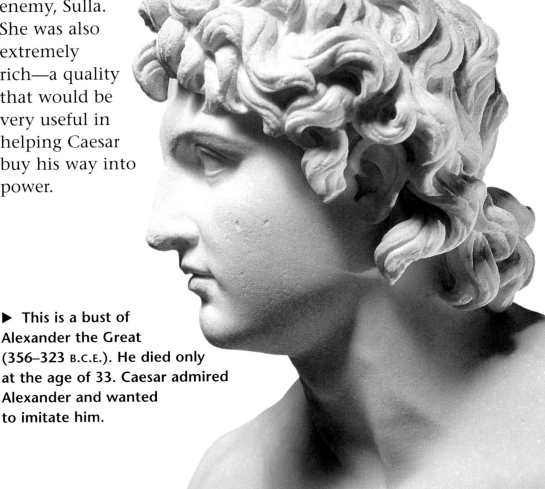

▶ This is a bust of Alexander the Great (356–323 B.C.E.). He died only at the age of 33. Caesar admired Alexander and wanted to imitate him.

The face of greatness

While Caesar was in Spain, he is said to have visited Cadiz. There he saw a statue of Alexander the Great. Caesar is reported to have sighed and said that by the time Alexander was his age he had achieved so much, but he himself had still not done anything of any real importance.

Climbing Up

Caesar could be very charming, and after he had returned to Rome from Spain, he set out to make friends in high places. One of these was a **senator** named Marcus Licinius Crassus, the richest man in Rome.

A new job

With the backing of his powerful new friends, Caesar was made *curule aedile* in 65 B.C.E. This was a very important post, placing him in charge of the upkeep of all the public buildings in Rome, as well as the organization of public entertainment. Caesar was now in the best position to win a lot of popularity and support from the people of Rome.

He asked his new friend Crassus to help him. With Crassus's money, Caesar was able to pay for huge public entertainments, organizing spectacular **gladiator** fights and magnificent religious festivals for the people of Rome. The city had never seen such wonderful displays. Many senators said that they were too expensive, but the people loved them.

▶ This terra-cotta statue shows two gladiators in action. The fight normally continued until one died, but a defeated gladiator could appeal for mercy.

Chief priest of Rome

Caesar's **political** career really took off in 63 B.C.E., when he was appointed *pontifex maximus,* or chief priest of Rome. He was not a religious man, but he was not going to let that prevent him from gaining yet more power. This new post was a power base from where he could plan his next move. Caesar was on the way up, and nothing was going to stop him.

◄ This coin shows Caesar wearing the veil of a chief priest.

Gladiator fights

Gladiators were prisoners, criminals, **slaves,** or paid volunteers who fought for the public's entertainment. They fought against each other or against wild animals. While he was *curule aedile,* Caesar organized a show that included 640 gladiators fighting each other, in one day alone.

Caesar and the Triumvirate

In July of 62 B.C.E., Caesar was elected to the important post of *praetor.* Two years later, he left Rome to become **governor** of the Roman **province** of Spain for a year. While he was there, he led a number of successful attacks on the local warriors. This added to his reputation back home and proved that he was a skilled military leader.

Back to politics

Caesar returned to Rome in 60 B.C.E. and went back to his **political** work. The great Roman general Pompey had also returned after military victories in the **Middle East.** Pompey had been so successful that the Roman **Senate** feared he was becoming too powerful. They decided not to give Pompey's soldiers the rewards of land that were customary after great victories. This was a huge insult to Pompey, who became very angry.

◀ This bronze statue of Caesar was probably made after he became a member of the **Triumvirate** in 60 B.C.E., when he was one of the most important people in Rome.

Caesar decided that this was his chance. He struck a deal with Pompey and Crassus. They agreed to support his bid to become one of the two **consuls** for the year 59 B.C.E. The post of consul was the most important political position in Rome. In return, Caesar promised to change certain laws to suit Pompey and Crassus. This agreement among the three men led them to become known as the Triumvirate.

Caesar becomes consul

Many officials were **bribed** by Crassus's money, and Caesar was soon elected as one of the two consuls. He immediately gave Pompey's soldiers their land and introduced new tax laws that enabled Crassus to become even richer. The Triumvirate members were now the most powerful men in Rome. No one dared challenge them.

▶ **This marble bust of Pompey shows him when he was a member of the Triumvirate.**

More weddings

In 62 B.C.E., Caesar divorced his second wife, Pompeia. His third wife was Calpurnia, the daughter of a rich senator named Calpurnius Piso. At the same time, Pompey married Caesar's daughter, Julia.

Caesar the Great General

A **consul** served for only a year, but when his term of office ended, he was entitled to become **governor** of one of Rome's **provinces**. With all his **bribes** and entertaining, Caesar was heavily in debt. He therefore needed to become governor of a very rich province. While he was still consul, he passed a law that meant he could become governor of not just one but three provinces: Cisalpine Gaul (now northern Italy), Transalpine Gaul (southern France), and Illyricum (Croatia).

An opportunity in Gaul

This new job was an opportunity to make lots of money, and the chance for Caesar to show off his skills as a great military leader. A huge Roman army was stationed in Gaul. When Caesar arrived there, the first thing he did was to make sure that the soldiers were well looked after, with good pay and food. This made him very popular with the men. He knew that one day he would be relying on their support.

▼ The carving on this Roman sarcophagus (stone coffin) shows a battle between the Romans and Gauls.

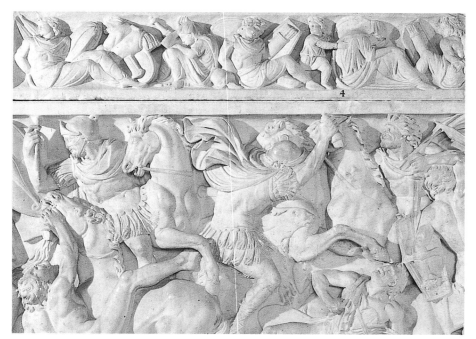

Two expeditions to Britain

Beyond Gaul lay the island of Britain. In the years 55 and 54 B.C.E., Caesar launched two unsuccessful invasions of Britain. However, with his usual skill, Caesar managed to present these failures as successes, making him even more popular among the Roman people.

Defeat of the Gauls

North of Transalpine Gaul, beyond the rule of Rome, lay the rich and fertile lands of northern France that were controlled by a number of **tribes**. In a **campaign** lasting two years, Caesar completely defeated these people and brought their lands under the direct rule of Rome. He made sure that his victories were reported back in Rome, so that everyone would know what a brilliant general he was.

▶ This statue is of Vercingetorix, leader of the Gauls of northern France. Julius Caesar finally defeated the Gauls in 51 B.C.E.

Who Will Rule?

While Caesar was away in Gaul, events in Rome were getting out of hand. Civic order was breaking down, and it was impossible to hold elections.

The old ruling families resented the enormous power held by the **Triumvirate**. Some **senators** believed that if they could get Pompey on their side, they would be able to break the Triumvirate's control. They began to spread rumors that Caesar's military successes were so great that he was now growing too powerful. This made Pompey, who thought of himself as the greatest of all the generals, very jealous.

The death of Crassus

As long as Crassus, the third member of the Triumvirate, remained in power, the situation would not boil over. But in 53 B.C.E., he was killed in battle. More riots broke out in Rome. Things were becoming so dangerous that the senators elected Pompey as **consul** to restore order. On Pompey's orders, the Senate asked Caesar to return to Rome to face charges of **corruption**.

▶ Marcus Tullius Cicero was a senator who supported the old **republican** system of government and was a bitter enemy of Julius Caesar. He was brutally murdered in 43 B.C.E.

The battle lines are drawn

Caesar was now in a tricky position. If he agreed to return to Rome, he would probably be killed. If he refused, he would be regarded as a criminal. He knew, however, that he had the support of his armies in Gaul. So the battle lines were now drawn for a **civil war** between his army and the Senate's army, led by Pompey.

▲ This seventeenth-century French painting by Jean Lemaire shows senators going to the Forum in Rome, where the main government buildings, including the Senate house, stood.

Breaking ties

Pompey could have chosen Caesar as the second consul. But he wanted to destroy Caesar, so instead he chose a senator named Metellus Scipio. Caesar's daughter, Julia, who had been married to Pompey, had died, and Pompey now married Scipio's daughter. The ties that had linked Pompey and Caesar were broken.

Crossing the Rubicon

In January of 49 B.C.E., Caesar and his army began to march toward Rome. They stopped when they reached the banks of the Rubicon River, the boundary that separated Gaul from Italy. Caesar knew that once he had crossed the river there would be no turning back. At this stage, he is supposed to have said, "The die is cast," meaning that he had to go on. He crossed into Italy and set out for Rome.

Pompey leaves Rome

As Caesar marched south, many more soldiers flocked to join him. Hearing news of this approaching danger, many **senators**, including Pompey, fled to Greece where another Roman army loyal to the Senate was stationed. Caesar was able to enter Rome without a fight, and he spent several months there preparing for his meeting with Pompey.

▶ Caesar and his army would have sailed to Greece in ships like the one on this coin. A Roman warship was powered by oars, pulled by **slaves** below the decks.

A battle in Greece

In 48 B.C.E., Caesar and his army sailed to Greece in pursuit of Pompey. On August 9, the two armies finally met. Even though he had many more soldiers in his army, Pompey was defeated. He fled from the battlefield to Egypt, where he had more friends and supporters.

Caesar sailed to Egypt a few weeks later. When he arrived there, he was met by some Egyptian messengers who presented him with the head of Pompey. The great general had already been murdered by his own men. His death made Caesar the undisputed leader of the Roman world.

▶ Egypt was ruled by King Ptolemy XIII and his sister Cleopatra. Caesar was greatly impressed by Cleopatra's beauty and intelligence.

Caesar and Cleopatra

Caesar helped Cleopatra to **depose** Ptolemy and become sole ruler of Egypt. Rumors soon spread that Caesar and Cleopatra were in love. This was probably true, and when Caesar returned to Rome, Cleopatra went with him. After Caesar's death, Cleopatra fell in love with the Roman **politician** Mark Antony.

Caesar the Dictator

Caesar remained in Egypt for nearly a year. His enemies were regrouping, though, and waiting for a chance to attack. In 47 B.C.E., Caesar defeated an Egyptian army led by Cleopatra's brother Ptolemy. Then he sailed to Spain, where he defeated Pompey's remaining followers at the Battle of Munda. The **civil war** was at an end, and Caesar could return to Rome in triumph. He was now about 54 years old.

Dictator for life

When he returned to Rome in 46 B.C.E., Caesar held four different victory celebrations. Soon after, he was also made **dictator** for life. The position of dictator was not new, but no one had been made dictator for life, and no dictator had ever been so powerful. Caesar stripped the **Senate** of its remaining powers, thus dealing the final blow to the old noble families who had ruled the **republic** for so long.

▶ When a Roman general returned from a successful **campaign**, he was allowed to hold a victory parade through Rome, called a Triumph. This picture by Andrea Mantegna, painted between 1486–94, shows a scene from one of Caesar's Triumphs.

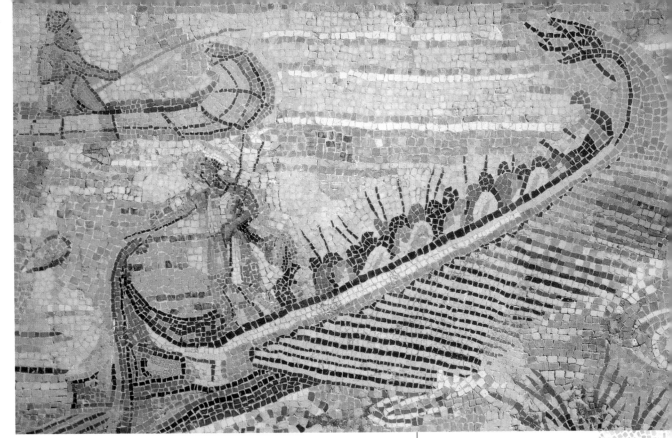

Total power

Caesar may have acted illegally in grabbing all this power for himself. In many ways, though, Rome and its territories were now much better governed than they had been for many years. The lives of many people, especially the common people at the bottom of society, were greatly improved.

▲ This pavement mosaic shows a Roman warship carrying soldiers down the Nile River in Egypt. Caesar was fascinated by the great wealth and ancient history of Egypt.

It is unlikely that Caesar had the welfare of his people in mind. The only person he really cared about was himself. His position as dictator was the prize he had won after years of careful planning and scheming. However, he did not enjoy his new powers for long.

A new calendar

The old Roman calendar was not very accurate. In 45 B.C.E., Caesar replaced it with a new calendar, now called the Julian calendar in his honor. It had 365 days in a year, with an extra day each fourth February to keep in line with the seasons. We still use this "leap year" system today.

One Demand Too Many

In 44 B.C.E., Julius Caesar seemed untouchable. But the old noble families that he had stripped of their traditional powers were just biding their time. A man with so much power inevitably had many enemies. The moment he slipped, they would pounce.

Caesar wants to be king

In March of 44 B.C.E., Caesar called a meeting of the **Senate** at which, it is claimed, he demanded that he should now be made king. This title would mean that when Caesar died, his adopted son would automatically become the next ruler.

The senators were horrified by this demand. It went against everything that Rome had stood for since the city's first kings had been expelled, more than 400 years earlier. Caesar's lust for power had gone too far—this was one demand too many.

Murdered in the Senate

A group of senators, led by Marcus Junius Brutus, started plotting against Caesar. On March 15, 44 B.C.E., Caesar went to the Senate to hear the response to his demand. Everyone rose to their feet as he entered the Senate house and walked to his throne at the end of the main chamber.

◄ This bronze Roman coin was made during Julius Caesar's rule as **dictator**. It bears his portrait and the **inscription**, "Caesar Dictator."

Then a group of senators, including Brutus, surrounded Caesar as if they were going to ask him questions. One of them suddenly pulled out a dagger and stabbed Caesar in the shoulder. All the others then fell on Caesar. He died almost immediately, falling to the ground at the base of the statue of his great rival, Pompey.

▲ Eighteenth-century Italian artist Vincenzo Camuccini painted this picture of Caesar being stabbed to death by the senators.

Beware the Ides *of March!*

A soothsayer—someone who predicts the future—had warned Caesar, "Beware the *Ides* of March!" The *Ides* was the fifteenth day of that month, and it fell on the day Caesar was to hear the Senate's reply. As he entered the Senate house, Caesar spotted the same soothsayer. Caesar is supposed to have said to the man that the *Ides* of March had come and he was unharmed, to which the soothsayer replied, "They have come, but they are not yet gone."

After Julius Caesar

As soon as news of Caesar's murder spread, street fighting and riots broke out in Rome. The senators abolished the **dictatorship** and tried to restore the old **republican** system of government. Others, including Caesar's great-nephew Octavian (whom Caesar had adopted as his own son at the beginning of 44 B.C.E.) and another **politician** named Mark Antony, opposed this return to power by the old **patrician** families.

▼ This tapestry, showing Caesar on horseback, was made about 1,500 years after his death. He was still regarded as one of the most important figures in history.

◀ When Octavian became emperor in 27 B.C.E., he was given the title of Augustus, meaning "revered one."

Civil war

Octavian and Mark Antony were supported by most of the common people of Rome and also by a large part of the Roman army. **Civil war** broke out between this group on one side and the **Senate** and the rest of the army on the other. In 42 B.C.E., the Senate was defeated. Nine years later, Octavian and Mark Antony fought against each other in yet another civil war. This time Mark Antony was defeated, and Octavian became the first Roman **emperor.** The change from a republic to an **empire**, begun by Julius Caesar, was now complete.

Caesar's legacy

Julius Caesar is one of the most important figures in history. The changes to the Roman system of government that he introduced remained in place for centuries after his death. His victories in Gaul led to the Roman conquest of much of northern Europe. This changed Rome from a power based around the Mediterranean Sea into a far greater European power.

In the end, Rome ruled one of the greatest empires the world had ever seen. The Roman language—Latin—and Roman ideas and skills dominated Europe and much of the **Middle East** for more than 500 years. Today, the Roman Empire that Julius Caesar helped to create is still seen as one of the world's greatest **civilizations.**

Glossary

ambition strong desire for success

astronomy scientific study of the sun, moon, planets, and stars

bribe money or goods offered in return for a service or favor

campaign series of operations, often military, to achieve a specific goal

citizen member of a state or nation

civilization highly developed, organized society

civil war war fought between groups within the same country

consul most senior Roman government official, in charge of the Senate and the army. Two consuls were elected each year.

corruption dishonest practices, such as bribery

culture shared ideas, beliefs, and values of a people

depose to remove from office or from a position of power

dictator person who takes sole control of the government and army in times of trouble, making all the political and military decisions

emperor ruler of an empire. The first Roman emperor was Augustus.

empire large land or group of lands ruled by one person or government

gladiator person who fought for the public's entertainment

governor official who ruled a province of the Roman Republic

Ides fifteenth day of March, May, July, or October, or the thirteenth day of each other month

inscription words carved into stone or on a coin

Middle East area around the eastern Mediterranean Sea, from Turkey to North Africa and eastward to Iran

monk man who is a member of a certain religious community

orator person who makes a speech in public

patrician member of the Roman upper class, descended from the oldest noble families. In early republican times, only patrician men could become senators.

philosophy study of the world, the purpose of the universe, and the nature of human life

piracy robbery on the seas; person who robs while on the seas is a pirate

politician person involved in government matters

politics business of government

praetor senior judge in ancient Rome

province area within an empire; for example, outside Rome but under Roman control

ransom payment of money for the release of a prisoner

republic state governed by people who are elected

scholar learned person

Senate group of officials, called senators, that governed Rome

slave servant who is the property of his or her master or mistress

talent ancient unit of money

tribe group of people, defined in terms of common descent, territory, and culture

tribune Roman elected by the people to represent them in the Senate

Triumvirate joint rule of Rome and its empire by three men: Caesar, Pompey, and Crassus

tutor teacher hired to teach a child at home

Time Line

By 264 B.C.E.	Rome becomes the most powerful state in Italy
About 100 B.C.E.	Birth of Julius Caesar
82–79 B.C.E.	Sulla rules as **dictator**
78 B.C.E.	Death of Sulla
70 B.C.E.	Marcus Crassus and Gnaeus Pompeius (Pompey) are **consuls**
59 B.C.E.	Caesar is made consul
58–50 B.C.E.	Caesar's **campaigns** in Gaul
53 B.C.E.	Death of Crassus
48 B.C.E.	Pompey is killed
45 B.C.E.	Caesar is named dictator for life
44 B.C.E.	Assassination of Julius Caesar
31 B.C.	Caesar's great-nephew and heir, Octavian, defeats Antony and Cleopatra at the Battle of Actium
27 B.C.E.	Octavian becomes the first Roman **emperor**, taking the title of Augustus. The Roman **Republic** becomes the Roman **Empire**.

Pronunciation Guide

Word	You say
Caesar	SEE-zer
curule aedile	KYOOR-ool EE-dile
Illyricum	ih-LEER-i-kum
Julii	JOO-lee-eye
Metellus Scipio	Me-TELL-us SIP-ee-oh
Minucius Thermus	Mi-NOO-she-us THER-mus
Pompeia	Pom-PEE-ah
praetor	PREE-ter
quaestor	QUEST-er
rhetor	REE-ter
sarcophagus	sar-KOFF-a-gus
Vercingetorix	Ver-sin-JET-or-ix

More Books to Read

Ganeri, Anita. *The Ancient Romans*. Austin, Tex.: Raintree Steck-Vaughn, 2000.
Langley, Andrew. *The Roman News*. Milwaukee, Wis.: Gareth Stevens, 2000.
Shuter, Jane. *The Ancient Romans*. Chicago: Heinemann Library, 1997.

Index